Digital Mindshift

How the Internet Rewires Our Brains.

Copyright Notice

Disclaimer

The information provided in this book, "Digital Mindshift: How the Internet Rewires Our Brains," is intended for general informational purposes only. While every effort has been made to ensure the accuracy and completeness of the information presented, the author and publisher assume no responsibility for errors or omissions, or for any results obtained from the use of the information contained in this book. Readers are encouraged to exercise their own judgment and seek professional advice if needed.

Contents

Introduction

Welcome to the era of the Digital Mindshift, a transformative journey into the very essence of our cognitive existence in the age of the internet.

In an era where our lives are intricately woven into the fabric of the digital realm, "Digital Mindshift: How the Internet Rewires Our Brains" invites you to embark on a compelling exploration of the profound impact that technology is having on the way we think, perceive, and interact with the world.

This book is an intellectual adventure into the uncharted territories of our evolving cognitive landscape.

As we navigate the vast and dynamic landscape of the internet, our brains are undergoing a metamorphosis, adapting to the rapid pace of information exchange and reshaping our fundamental cognitive processes.

The pages that follow will unravel the mysteries of how the internet, with its boundless connectivity and endless streams of information, is rewiring the neural pathways that define our humanity.

We will delve into the ways in which the digital age has altered our attention spans, transformed our memory retention, and even redefined the nature of creativity itself.

Far from succumbing to sensationalism, "Digital Mindshift" seeks to strike a delicate balance between acknowledging the potential benefits of our digital interconnectedness and addressing the challenges it poses to our cognitive well-being.

By drawing on the latest research in neuroscience, psychology, and technology, The author paints a nuanced portrait of the evolving relationship between our brains and the internet.

This book is an invitation to question, to reflect, and to understand the intricate dance between the virtual and the neural. Whether you're a fervent advocate for the limitless possibilities of the digital age or a cautious skeptic concerned about its consequences, "Digital Mindshift" is your compass in navigating the uncharted waters of the internet's influence on our minds.

Let's embark on a thought-provoking journey that transcends the binary narratives of optimism and alarmism, and explore the profound implications of the Digital Mindshift.

It's time to rethink the way we perceive ourselves in this digital landscape and to appreciate the power and potential pitfalls that come with the rewiring of our very minds.

Chapter 1

The Neuroplastic Web: How Our Brain Adapts

In the ever-evolving landscape of the digital age, our brains are navigating a vast and intricate network of information – the neuroplastic web.

Neuroplasticity, a term that refers to the brain's ability to reorganize itself by forming new neural connections, is a phenomenon that holds profound implications for our understanding of human cognition.

This chapter delves into the fascinating concept of neuroplasticity, with a particular focus on how the brain reshapes itself in response to the myriad online activities that have become integral to our daily lives.

Unraveling Neuroplasticity

Neuroplasticity, also known as brain plasticity, is a fascinating and dynamic property of the brain that refers to its ability to reorganize itself by forming new neural connections throughout life.

This intricate process plays a crucial role in learning, memory, and recovery from brain injuries.

The concept of neuroplasticity challenges the traditional view that the brain is a static and fixed organ, highlighting its remarkable adaptability in response to various experiences and stimuli.

At the core of neuroplasticity is the ability of neurons, the fundamental building blocks of the nervous system, to undergo structural and functional changes.

This occurs through mechanisms such as synaptic plasticity, where the strength and efficiency of connections between neurons, known as synapses, can be altered.

Long-term potentiation (LTP) and long-term depression (LTD) are two well-studied forms of synaptic plasticity that contribute to the strengthening or weakening of these connections, respectively.

Environmental stimuli, learning experiences, and sensory input play pivotal roles in driving neuroplastic changes.

For instance, when an individual engages in a new skill or acquires new knowledge, the brain adapts by forming new synapses or reinforcing existing ones.

This process is often associated with changes in the density of dendritic spines, small protrusions on neurons that receive synaptic input. The structural modifications occurring at the microscopic level translate into macroscopic changes in brain function. Neuroplasticity is not only evident in the healthy, developing brain but also plays a crucial role in the recovery from brain injuries.

Following trauma or stroke, the brain can undergo extensive reorganization to compensate for lost functions.

This phenomenon, known as functional recovery or brain rewiring, involves the recruitment of undamaged neural pathways to take on the functions of the damaged ones.

Rehabilitation strategies harness neuroplasticity to enhance recovery by promoting the establishment of alternative neural circuits.

Understanding neuroplasticity has profound implications for fields such as education, rehabilitation, and mental health.

Educational approaches that leverage neuroplasticity principles can optimize learning outcomes, while therapeutic interventions can be designed to exploit the brain's ability to reorganize itself for recovery after injury or in the treatment of neurological disorders.

Moreover, ongoing research in neuroplasticity opens new avenues for developing innovative interventions and technologies aimed at enhancing cognitive abilities and overall brain health across the lifespan.

This adaptability is not only limited to physical experiences but extends to the virtual realm, where online activities play a prominent role.

The Digital Tapestry: Online Activities and Neuroplasticity

The digital era has woven a complex and interconnected landscape known as the "digital tapestry," where individuals engage in a myriad of online activities that shape their cognitive experiences.

In this vast virtual realm, the impact of online activities on neuroplasticity is an intriguing subject of exploration.

The constant interaction with digital platforms, social media, and online content has the potential to influence the brain's structure and function, giving rise to a new frontier in the understanding of neuroplasticity.

One aspect of the digital tapestry that

intersects with neuroplasticity is the phenomenon of digital learning.

Educational platforms, online courses, and interactive learning materials have become integral components of modern education.

Engaging with digital learning environments often requires adaptive cognitive processes, promoting synaptic plasticity as individuals acquire and assimilate new information.

The flexibility of online learning activities may enhance neuroplasticity by providing varied stimuli and learning modalities.

Social media, another prominent feature of the digital tapestry, introduces a social dimension to online activities.

The constant interaction with diverse

content and the engagement with social networks can shape social cognition and emotional regulation.

Neuroplastic changes may occur as individuals navigate the intricate web of online relationships, adapting their neural circuits to the demands of virtual social interactions.

However, the impact of social media on neuroplasticity is a double-edged sword, with both positive and negative consequences depending on the nature and quality of online engagement.

The omnipresence of digital entertainment, such as video games, streaming services, and interactive content, adds another layer to the digital tapestry.

Video games, in particular, have been studied for their potential influence on cognitive abilities and neuroplasticity.

The interactive and immersive nature of gaming experiences may stimulate specific neural pathways, potentially leading to adaptive changes in the brain.

However, the impact of digital entertainment on neuroplasticity remains a subject of ongoing research, with debates about the long-term consequences of excessive screen time.

As individuals navigate the digital tapestry, it is essential to consider the implications of online activities on mental health.

Excessive use of social media, information overload, and the constant bombardment of stimuli may contribute to cognitive fatigue and potential negative effects on mental well-being.

Understanding how the digital environment interacts with neuroplasticity can guide the development of interventions that promote positive online experiences and mitigate potential risks associated with prolonged digital engagement.

Chapter 2

Scrolling Through Synapses: Social Media's Influence

In the digital age, social media has become an omnipresent force, shaping the way we perceive the world and interact with others.

This chapter delves into the intricate relationship between social media and the human psyche, exploring the profound psychological effects that scrolling through social media platforms can have on our thoughts, emotions, and social interactions.

The Evolution of Social Interaction

Social interaction has undergone profound transformations throughout human history, shaped by advancements in communication, technology, and cultural dynamics.

In the early stages of human civilization, face-to-face interactions were the primary mode of communication, essential for survival and community cohesion.

These interactions were characterized by proximity, non-verbal cues, and a direct exchange of information, fostering a deep sense of interpersonal connection within small, close-knit groups.

The invention of written language marked a significant milestone in the evolution of social interaction, enabling the preservation and transmission of knowledge beyond the constraints of oral communication.

As societies developed, so did the methods of communication, with written letters, scrolls, and eventually printed materials serving as mediums for sharing information and ideas across greater distances.

This expansion of communication tools laid the groundwork for more complex and interconnected social structures.

The advent of the telegraph and telephone in the 19th century further revolutionized social interaction by allowing near-instantaneous communication over long distances.

The ability to hear the voice of a loved one or receive news from afar in real-time brought about a sense of immediacy and intimacy that transcended geographic boundaries.

However, these technologies still relied on voice and text, preserving some aspects of traditional communication.

The late 20th century witnessed a seismic shift with the rise of the internet, ushering in a new era of social interaction.

Email, online forums, and chat rooms provided virtual spaces for communication, breaking down barriers of time and space.

The emergence of social media platforms in the 21st century took this evolution to another level, transforming the nature of social interactions.

Platforms like Facebook, X (Twitter), and Instagram allowed individuals to share their lives, opinions, and experiences on a global scale, fostering virtual communities and shaping online identities.

The evolution of social interaction continues with the integration of advanced technologies such as video calls, virtual reality, and augmented reality.

These innovations offer immersive and interactive experiences that simulate face-to-face interactions, even when individuals are physically distant.

The COVID-19 pandemic accelerated the adoption of these technologies, highlighting their potential to maintain social connections during times of physical isolation.

However, the evolution of social interaction is not without challenges. The digital realm brings issues of privacy, misinformation, and the potential for social isolation. Balancing the benefits of global connectivity with the preservation of authentic, meaningful connections remains a critical consideration.

The Dopamine Dance: Reward Systems at Play

The addictive nature of social media is intricately tied to the constant cycle of reward and anticipation woven into its design.

Social media platforms employ sophisticated algorithms and user interfaces that exploit fundamental principles of behavioral psychology, creating a potent psychological loop that keeps users engaged and craving more.

At the heart of this loop is the intermittent reinforcement of rewards, a mechanism that has long been recognized as a powerful driver of addictive behaviors.

Social media platforms leverage the concept of variable rewards, wherein users are uncertain about the nature, timing, and magnitude of the rewards they might receive.

This unpredictability triggers a heightened state of arousal and anticipation, as individuals continually check their notifications or scroll through their feeds in the hope of encountering something rewarding—be it a like, comment, or share. The intermittent nature of these rewards, coupled with the social validation they provide, leads to the activation of the brain's reward system, specifically the release of dopamine, a neurotransmitter associated with pleasure and reinforcement.

The anticipation of rewards on social media creates a psychological loop that reinforces the behavior of using these platforms.

The brain learns to associate the act of checking notifications or posting content with the possibility of receiving positive feedback.

This learned association strengthens over time, making the behavior more habitual and difficult to break.

Users find themselves caught in a continuous loop of seeking and anticipating rewards, perpetuating their engagement with social media in a compulsive manner.

The gamification elements embedded in social media platforms further amplify the addictive nature of the experience.

Features such as likes, comments, and follower counts are quantifiable metrics that turn online interactions into a measurable game.

The pursuit of higher numbers and social validation becomes a goal in itself, compelling users to continually participate in the social media environment to accrue these digital rewards.

The psychological satisfaction derived from achieving these milestones reinforces the addictive loop, driving individuals to spend increasing amounts of time on these platforms.

The addictive nature of social media is also exacerbated by the personalized nature of content delivery.

Algorithms analyze user behavior and preferences to curate content tailored to individual interests, ensuring that each interaction is potentially rewarding.

This personalized experience creates a sense of exclusivity and relevance, further deepening the psychological connection and reinforcing the addictive loop.

The Social Comparison Conundrum

The social comparison conundrum is a psychological phenomenon that reflects the pervasive tendency of individuals to assess their own abilities, achievements, and well-being in relation to those of others.

Rooted in social psychology, social comparison theory posits that people determine their own social and personal worth based on how they stack up against others in their social environment.

While social comparison is a natural and common human behavior, the conundrum arises from the potential negative consequences associated with constant comparisons in the context of social interactions, particularly in the era of social media.

In the age of digital connectivity, social media platforms provide a fertile ground for the social comparison conundrum to flourish. Individuals are exposed to curated representations of others' lives, often showcasing their achievements, vacations, relationships, and other positive aspects.

The constant exposure to these idealized images can lead to upward social comparison, where individuals perceive themselves as inferior or less successful than their peers.

This can contribute to feelings of inadequacy, low self-esteem, and a sense of not measuring up to societal standards.

Conversely, social media can also foster downward social comparison, where individuals may feel a temporary boost in self-esteem by comparing themselves to others whom they perceive as less successful or fortunate.

However, this form of comparison is not without its pitfalls, as it can lead to a false sense of superiority and, in the long run, contribute to a negative social environment.

The social comparison conundrum extends beyond the digital realm and can manifest in various aspects of life, including work, education, and personal relationships.

In the workplace, for example, employees may compare their achievements, salaries, or career progression to their colleagues, influencing job satisfaction and motivation. In educational settings, students may compare their grades or academic performance, impacting their self-esteem and study habits.

Emotional Contagion in the Digital Realm

Emotional contagion, the phenomenon where one person's emotions and related behaviors can influence or "infect" others, is a well-established concept in psychology. In the digital realm, emotional contagion takes on new dimensions, as individuals engage with content and interact through various online platforms.

Social media, in particular, plays a significant role in amplifying emotional contagion, shaping the emotional experiences of users and creating a virtual environment where emotions can spread rapidly.

Social media platforms are designed to facilitate the sharing of emotions, experiences, and opinions. When users encounter emotionally charged content, whether it be positive or negative, they are more likely to experience and express similar emotions.

The rapid dissemination of emotional content through likes, shares, and comments creates a ripple effect, with emotions spreading across networks in a way that mirrors real-world social interactions.

This can contribute to the collective mood of online communities, creating a digital echo chamber where emotions intensify and resonate.

The algorithms employed by social media platforms further enhance emotional contagion by tailoring content to individual preferences and engagement patterns.

Users are more likely to be exposed to content that aligns with their existing emotional states and preferences, creating a feedback loop that reinforces and amplifies specific emotions.

This personalized content delivery can lead to emotional homogeneity within online communities, as individuals are exposed to a narrow range of perspectives and emotional experiences.

While positive emotional contagion can foster a sense of community and shared joy, the dark side of this phenomenon becomes apparent in the spread of negative emotions.

The rapid dissemination of fear, anger, or sadness through viral content can contribute to the amplification of emotional distress on a large scale.

Misinformation, divisive content, and sensationalism can fuel negative emotional contagion, influencing public discourse and contributing to a polarized digital landscape.

Chapter 3

Click, Dopamine, Repeat: The Addiction Loop

In the digital age, online platforms have become ubiquitous, seamlessly woven into the fabric of our daily lives.

This chapter delves into the captivating yet concerning phenomenon of the addiction loop, exploring how online platforms exploit the brain's reward system, particularly the role of dopamine, to shape and perpetuate addictive behaviors.

The Dopamine Connection

The Dopamine Connection has become a central aspect of the digital landscape, particularly on online platforms.

These platforms have intricately woven the understanding of human psychology, specifically the role of dopamine, into their design to create an environment that maximizes user engagement.

Dopamine, often referred to as the "feel-good" neurotransmitter, is associated with pleasure, reward, and motivation.

Online platforms leverage this physiological response by engineering an environment where each click, like, or notification prompts a surge of dopamine, reinforcing the user's engagement.

In the realm of social media, the anticipation of positive feedback in the form of likes, comments, or shares triggers the release of dopamine.

When users post content, they are essentially seeking validation, and the instant feedback loop provided by these platforms satisfies the innate human desire for social recognition.

The unpredictable nature of this feedback, akin to a variable reward system, intensifies the dopamine release, creating a sense of excitement and addiction.

Similarly, the concept of infinite scrolling on platforms like Instagram, X, or Facebook is a deliberate strategy to keep users engaged for longer periods.

As users scroll through a continuous feed of content, each new piece becomes a potential source of reward, be it an interesting article, a captivating image, or a humorous meme.

This constant stream of stimuli maintains an ongoing dopamine release, making it challenging for users to disengage voluntarily.

Notifications also play a pivotal role in the dopamine-driven engagement cycle. The "ping" of a new message, like, or mention serves as a direct reward, prompting users to check their devices immediately.

The intermittent reinforcement of notifications, sometimes referred to as a "digital slot machine," capitalizes on the unpredictability of the reward, compelling users to repeatedly check for updates in anticipation of a positive interaction.

The implications of the Dopamine Connection extend beyond mere user engagement; it raises ethical considerations regarding the design of digital platforms.

Critics argue that the intentional engineering of addictive features exploits human psychology for profit, leading to concerns about the impact on mental health and well-being.

As users become increasingly aware of the dopamine-driven nature of online interactions, there is a growing call for responsible design practices that prioritize user health over maximizing screen time.

The Instant Gratification Paradigm

The Instant Gratification Paradigm has become a hallmark of online platforms, shaping user experiences and behaviors in profound ways.

These platforms are meticulously designed to provide a quick and satisfying response to user actions, fostering a sense of immediacy and reward.

At the core of this paradigm is the understanding that modern users, accustomed to the fast-paced nature of the digital age, crave instant results and responses.

Online platforms employ a variety of features to cater to the desire for instant gratification.

One notable example is the instantaneous loading of content. Whether it's a webpage, a social media feed, or a video streaming service, platforms prioritize reducing loading times to ensure that users can access information swiftly.

This swift response to user input creates a seamless and responsive digital experience, keeping users engaged and satisfied.

The design of user interfaces also plays a crucial role in the Instant Gratification Paradigm. Intuitive interfaces that respond promptly to user interactions contribute to a feeling of control and efficiency.

For example, the use of feedback animations, such as a "like" button changing color or a message being sent with a satisfying animation, reinforces the idea that the platform is responsive to the user's actions.

The concept of one-click actions is another manifestation of the Instant Gratification Paradigm. Online shopping platforms, for instance, have streamlined the purchasing process to a single click, minimizing the steps required between desire and fulfillment.

This simplicity not only caters to users' impatience but also serves the business model by encouraging quick and frequent transactions.

In the realm of social media, the scroll and swipe functionalities epitomize instant gratification. Users can effortlessly navigate through a continuous stream of content with a simple flick of the finger, providing a constant flow of stimuli.

The design of these platforms capitalizes on the human instinct to seek novelty, ensuring that users are continuously presented with fresh and engaging content to maintain their interest.

Social Validation and FOMO

Social validation and the Fear of Missing Out (FOMO) are powerful psychological phenomena that significantly influence behavior in the digital age, especially on social media platforms.

Social validation refers to the human tendency to seek approval, recognition, and affirmation from others. In the context of online interactions, features like likes, comments, and shares serve as visible forms of social validation.

Users often gauge the perceived popularity or acceptance of their posts through these metrics, and the positive feedback received triggers a sense of validation, satisfaction, and a release of dopamine, reinforcing the desire for continued engagement.

FOMO, on the other hand, is characterized by the apprehension that others are enjoying experiences from which one is absent.

Social media platforms, with their real-time updates and constant stream of curated content, play a significant role in exacerbating FOMO.

Users witness their peers engaging in activities, social events, or even online conversations, leading to a heightened sense of missing out on rewarding experiences.

The fear of being left out creates a sense of urgency and compels individuals to stay connected, refreshing feeds and checking notifications to alleviate the anxiety associated with potentially missing something important or enjoyable.

These two phenomena often intertwine on social media platforms, creating a loop of behaviors that contribute to addictive usage patterns.

The pursuit of social validation, manifested in the form of likes and comments, becomes a driving force to share more, seek more attention, and stay actively involved in the platform.

Simultaneously, the fear of missing out intensifies the need for continuous monitoring, as users strive to stay updated on the activities and experiences of their social circle.

Escalation of Engagement

The Escalation of Engagement is a phenomenon observed in online platforms, where users, initially drawn in by the appeal of content, find themselves ensnared in an addiction loop.

As users engage with content, platforms meticulously track their behaviors and preferences.

This wealth of data becomes the fuel for sophisticated algorithms that aim to tailor the user experience, creating a personalized and addictive environment.

This escalation is driven by the platforms' desire to maximize user engagement, as increased time spent on the platform translates into more opportunities for advertisements and other revenue-generating activities.

Moreover, the implementation of features like autoplay, suggested content, and infinite scrolling plays a crucial role in the escalation of engagement.

These features eliminate natural stopping points, encouraging users to continue consuming content without conscious decisions to disengage.

The seamless transition from one piece of content to the next keeps users immersed, contributing to the addictive nature of the platform.

The use of notifications is another key element in the escalation of engagement.

Online platforms strategically employ push notifications to draw users back into the platform by alerting them to new content, updates, or interactions.

The anticipation created by these notifications, coupled with the element of surprise and unpredictability, contributes to the addictive cycle, prompting users to check their devices frequently and stay connected.

The Toll on Mental Well-being

The addictive nature of online platforms has become a significant concern, raising profound questions about its impact on mental well-being.

The addiction loop, a product of clever platform design, is a series of triggers and rewards designed to keep users engaged and coming back for more.

While this design strategy may be a testament to the ingenuity of developers, it comes with serious implications for the mental health of users.

1 **Constant Connectivity and Overstimulation:** Online platforms are designed to keep users connected constantly, fostering an environment of overstimulation.

The constant influx of information, notifications, and updates can overwhelm individuals, leading to stress and anxiety.

The need to stay connected at all times can disrupt sleep patterns and contribute to chronic stress, which is detrimental to mental well-being.

2 **Comparison and Social Pressure:** Social media platforms, in particular, contribute to the comparison culture, where users constantly measure their lives against the

curated highlights of others.

This can lead to feelings of inadequacy, low self-esteem, and depression. The pressure to conform to societal expectations and maintain a certain online image can take a toll on mental health.

3 **Time Distortion and Productivity Loss:**
The addictive nature of online platforms can distort users' perception of time.

Hours can pass unnoticed as individuals scroll through endless feeds or engage in online activities.

This can lead to a loss of productivity, impacting personal and professional responsibilities, and subsequently causing stress and guilt.

4 **Cyberbullying and Online Harassment:**
Online platforms provide a space for
cyberbullying and harassment,
contributing to significant mental health
issues.

The anonymity and distance provided by
the online environment can embolden
individuals to engage in harmful
behaviors, causing emotional distress and
trauma for the victims.

5 **FOMO (Fear of Missing Out):** The
constant stream of updates on social
media can trigger FOMO, causing
individuals to feel anxious or left out if
they are not actively participating.

This fear of missing out can lead to
compulsive checking of social media,

further contributing to the addictive nature of online platforms.

6 **Reduced Face-to-Face Interaction:** Excessive use of online platforms can lead to a decline in face-to-face interactions.

Human connections and relationships are essential for mental well-being, and the isolation resulting from excessive screen time can contribute to feelings of loneliness and depression.

7 **Privacy Concerns and Stress:** The awareness of constant surveillance and the potential misuse of personal data can contribute to heightened stress levels.

The erosion of privacy in the online space can lead to a sense of vulnerability and unease, negatively impacting mental health.

Chapter 4

Information Overload: Coping with the Flood of Data

In the digital age, we find ourselves swimming in an ocean of information, with an incessant flood of data coming from various sources.

This chapter delves into the challenges posed by information overload, exploring how the sheer volume of data impacts our attention spans, decision-making processes, and overall cognitive well-being.

The Digital Deluge

The Digital Deluge refers to the overwhelming and ever-increasing volume of digital data that is generated, transmitted, and stored on a global scale.

This phenomenon is a direct consequence of the rapid advancement of technology, particularly in the realms of computing, communication, and information storage.

The deluge encompasses a wide range of data types, including text, images, videos, and more, creating a complex landscape that poses both challenges and opportunities for individuals, businesses, and society at large.

One aspect of the Digital Deluge is the exponential growth of data production.

With the proliferation of internet-connected devices, social media platforms, and online services, individuals and organizations are constantly generating vast amounts of data.

This includes everything from social interactions and personal preferences to business transactions and scientific research.

The sheer scale of this data generation presents challenges related to storage, processing, and analysis, necessitating the development of advanced technologies and strategies to harness its potential.

Moreover, the Digital Deluge has given rise to the concept of big data, where datasets are so massive and complex that traditional data processing methods are inadequate.

The ability to extract meaningful insights from these vast datasets has become a critical skill for businesses and researchers.

Data analytics, machine learning, and artificial intelligence are among the tools employed to sift through and derive value from the digital deluge, offering new possibilities for innovation, decision-making, and problem-solving.

However, alongside the opportunities, the Digital Deluge raises concerns about privacy, security, and ethical considerations.

The massive collection and storage of personal data have raised questions about how that information is used, who has access to it, and the potential for misuse.

On the other hand, cybersecurity threats and data breaches pose significant risks, highlighting the need for robust measures to safeguard digital information and ensure the integrity of digital systems.

Attention Span Erosion

The advent of the digital age has ushered in an era of unprecedented access to information, but with it comes the concern of attention span erosion.

As the volume of information vying for our attention continues to increase, individuals find themselves navigating a constant barrage of stimuli from various sources, such as social media, news outlets, and online platforms.

This influx of information contributes to a diminishing attention span, as individuals become accustomed to consuming bite-sized, rapidly changing content.

In this era of information overload, the demand for quick and engaging content has given rise to platforms designed for rapid consumption.

Social media platforms, in particular, thrive on the delivery of succinct and visually appealing content that can capture attention within seconds.

This shift towards shorter attention spans is driven by the need to compete in a crowded digital landscape where numerous messages are vying for the limited attention of users.

The consequences of attention span erosion extend beyond the realm of entertainment and social media.

In educational settings and professional environments, individuals may find it increasingly challenging to focus on lengthy texts or complex tasks.

The expectation for immediate and concise information has the potential to impact critical thinking skills and the ability to delve deeply into complex topics.

Moreover, the constant need for novelty and instant gratification can lead to a culture of distraction, where individuals are more prone to multitasking and switching between tasks rapidly.

This constant switching can hinder deep cognitive processing and sustained attention, impacting the quality of work and overall productivity.

Decision Paralysis in the Information Jungle

The Information Jungle, characterized by the vast and intricate network of data available in the digital age, has brought about a phenomenon known as Decision Paralysis.

As the volume and variety of information continue to surge, individuals find themselves overwhelmed by choices and data points, making decision-making a daunting task.

This inundation of information often leads to a state of indecision, where individuals struggle to process and evaluate the abundance of options before them.

One of the primary contributors to Decision Paralysis is the sheer magnitude of available information.

From product reviews and expert opinions to user-generated content and diverse perspectives, the range of data can be paralyzing.

The fear of making the wrong decision amid this wealth of information can cause individuals to postpone or avoid decisions altogether.

This hesitancy is particularly evident in online shopping, where an extensive array of products and reviews can create a sense of uncertainty, hindering the ability to make a confident choice.

Moreover, the rapid pace at which information evolves in the Information Jungle adds another layer of complexity.

The fear of missing out on the latest and most relevant data can lead to procrastination and a perpetual cycle of information-seeking.

The constant influx of updates and new insights can make individuals reluctant to commit to a decision, as they anticipate that newer and better information may emerge shortly.

In professional and personal spheres alike, Decision Paralysis can have tangible consequences.

In business, for example, leaders may struggle to choose the best strategies or investments amid an ever-changing landscape of data and market trends.

In personal life, individuals may grapple with choices ranging from career decisions to everyday purchases, impacting their overall well-being and satisfaction.

Stress and Cognitive Fatigue

The constant bombardment of information in the digital age has become a pervasive aspect of daily life, and its impact on mental well-being is profound.

The relentless stream of notifications, emails, social media updates, and news alerts places individuals in a perpetual state of connectivity, leaving little room for mental rest.

The overwhelming volume of information demands attention and cognitive processing, contributing to a heightened state of arousal and vigilance.

This constant stimulation can lead to heightened stress levels as individuals grapple with the challenge of filtering and processing information to make meaningful decisions.

The barrage of information not only induces stress but also contributes significantly to cognitive fatigue.

As individuals navigate a sea of data, the brain is forced to continuously switch between tasks, process new information, and make decisions.

This cognitive load, compounded by the rapid pace at which information is presented, can overwhelm the brain's capacity for sustained attention and thoughtful processing.

Over time, this cognitive fatigue manifests as a decline in mental sharpness, reduced ability to focus, and an overall feeling of mental exhaustion.

Moreover, the content of the information itself can contribute to stress.

The constant exposure to negative news, alarming headlines, and distressing images can heighten anxiety and contribute to a sense of helplessness.

The fear of missing out (FOMO) and the pressure to stay informed can also drive individuals to consume information compulsively, exacerbating stress levels and cognitive fatigue.

Signs of Information Overload

Information overload occurs when an individual is exposed to more information than they can effectively process, leading to feelings of overwhelm and difficulty in making decisions. Here are some signs that may indicate information overload:

1 **Difficulty in Decision-Making:** When faced with too much information, individuals may find it challenging to make decisions. The abundance of

options and data can lead to decision paralysis.

2 **Feeling Overwhelmed:** A sense of being overwhelmed or stressed due to the sheer volume of information can be a clear sign of information overload. This may manifest as anxiety, frustration, or a feeling of helplessness.

3 **Reduced Productivity:** Information overload can hinder productivity. When there's too much data to sift through, it becomes harder to focus on essential tasks and priorities, resulting in decreased overall productivity.

4 **Increased Distractions:** Excessive information can lead to increased distractions. Constant notifications,

emails, or messages may make it difficult to concentrate on a single task for an extended period.

5 **Memory Issues:** Information overload can affect memory retention. With an overwhelming amount of information to process, individuals may struggle to remember key details or recall information when needed.

6 **Physical Symptoms:** Information overload can have physical manifestations such as headaches, eye strain, and fatigue. These symptoms can be a result of prolonged exposure to screens or the stress associated with processing large amounts of information.

7 **Incomplete Tasks:** Difficulty in completing tasks is another sign. When overwhelmed with information, individuals may start multiple tasks without finishing them, leading to a sense of unproductivity.

8 **Constant Connectivity:** The need to stay constantly connected to information sources, such as emails, social media, and news feeds, may indicate information overload. The fear of missing out (FOMO) can contribute to this constant need for updates.

9 **Neglecting Personal Well-Being:** Information overload can lead to neglecting personal well-being, as individuals may spend excessive time

consuming information at the expense of activities like exercise, relaxation, or socializing.

10 **Inability to Filter Relevant Information:** Difficulty in filtering and discerning relevant information from irrelevant or less important details is a common sign. This can lead to the consumption of information that may not contribute meaningfully to one's goals or decision-making processes.

Chapter 5

Coping Strategies: Navigating the Information Landscape

Effectively navigating the information landscape requires the development of coping strategies to manage information overload. These strategies encompass both individual practices and societal approaches. Some key strategies include:

Mindful Consumption

Mindful consumption refers to the intentional and conscious approach to consuming information, media, and content.

In the context of navigating the information landscape, where there is a constant influx of data from various sources, practicing mindful consumption can be a valuable coping strategy.

Here are some ways in which mindful consumption can be applied as a coping strategy:

1 **Awareness of Information Overload:** Mindful consumption involves recognizing when you are experiencing information overload.

This awareness allows you to take a step back and assess whether you need to continue consuming information at the current pace or if it's time to take a break.

2 **Quality over Quantity:** Instead of mindlessly scrolling through vast amounts of information, prioritize the quality of the content.

Focus on reputable sources, well-researched articles, and information that adds value to your understanding.

3 **Scheduled Information Breaks:** Designate specific times for information consumption.

This could involve setting aside dedicated periods during the day to catch up on news, social media, or other sources.

Outside of these designated times, limit exposure to reduce the risk of information overload.

4 **Balanced Media Diet:** Consciously diversify your sources of information. Engage with content that offers different perspectives and avoid echo chambers. This helps in developing a more comprehensive understanding of issues.

5 **Mindful Social Media Use:** Social media can be a significant source of information, but it can also contribute to stress and anxiety. Be mindful of your social media use, curate your feeds, and consider taking breaks to maintain a healthy balance.

6 **Critical Evaluation:** Develop critical thinking skills to evaluate the information you encounter.

Question the sources, check for biases, and verify facts before accepting information as accurate.

This approach can help you avoid misinformation and make more informed decisions.

7 **Setting Boundaries:** Establish clear boundaries for information consumption. This may involve turning off notifications, designating device-free times, or creating specific spaces in your home where you disconnect from digital information.

8 **Mindful Engagement:** When engaging with content, be present in the moment. Avoid multitasking and give your full attention to the information you are consuming.

This not only enhances comprehension but also reduces the likelihood of feeling overwhelmed.

9 **Digital Detox:** Periodically disconnect from digital devices to recharge. Engage in activities that promote relaxation and well-being, such as exercise, nature walks, or mindfulness practices. This helps in reducing stress associated with constant information exposure.

10 **Reflective Practices:** Take time to reflect on your emotional and mental responses to the information you consume. Understand how certain types of content impact your well-being, and adjust your consumption habits accordingly.

Digital Detox

Digital detox refers to a period during which an individual refrains from using digital devices and technology.

This intentional break from the digital world can be a valuable coping strategy in navigating the information landscape, especially when the constant influx of information can lead to stress, burnout, and feelings of being overwhelmed.

Here are some tips on how to achieve a digital detox:

1 **Set Clear Intentions:** Clearly define the purpose and duration of your digital detox. Whether it's a day, a weekend, or longer, having a clear goal will help you stay committed.

2 **Inform Others:** Let friends, family, and colleagues know about your digital detox in advance. This helps manage expectations and reduces the likelihood of feeling pressured to respond to digital communications.

3 **Establish Boundaries:** Create physical and temporal boundaries for your digital detox. Consider turning off notifications, setting specific times for device use, or designating device-free zones in your home.

4 **Plan Alternative Activities:** Identify alternative activities that you can engage in during your digital detox. This could include reading a book, spending time in nature, practicing mindfulness or

meditation, or pursuing a hobby.

5 **Unplug Gradually:** If a complete digital detox feels challenging, consider unplugging gradually. Start by reducing screen time, limiting social media use, or taking short breaks from specific devices before committing to a more extended detox.

6 **Create a Support System:** Engage friends or family members in your digital detox journey. Having a support system can make the experience more enjoyable and provide accountability.

7 **Use Technology Mindfully:** During non-detox times, practice mindful and intentional use of technology. Be aware of the time you spend on devices, and

use them with a purpose rather than out of habit.

8 **Digital-Free Bedrooms:** Keep your bedroom a technology-free zone. Avoid using electronic devices right before bedtime to improve sleep quality and overall well-being.

9 **Explore Offline Hobbies:** Rediscover or explore hobbies that don't involve digital devices. Whether it's painting, cooking, playing a musical instrument, or engaging in sports, offline activities can provide a welcome break.

10 **Reflect and Journal:** Use the digital detox as an opportunity for self-reflection. Journaling about your experiences, thoughts, and emotions during this time

can help you gain insights into your relationship with technology.

11 **Embrace Nature:** Spend time outdoors and connect with nature. Whether it's a hike, a walk in the park, or simply sitting in a garden, nature can have a calming effect and provide a refreshing perspective.

12 **Focus on Face-to-Face Interactions:** Prioritize face-to-face interactions with friends and family. Use the time away from screens to strengthen real-world connections.

Remember that the key to a successful digital detox is finding a balance that works for you. It's not about completely eliminating technology from your life but rather establishing a healthy relationship with it.

By periodically disconnecting, you can recharge, reduce stress, and approach the digital world with a refreshed perspective.

Technology-Assisted Solutions

Technology-assisted solutions play a significant role in helping individuals navigate the information landscape, especially in the face of information overload, rapidly changing content, and the proliferation of digital platforms.

Leveraging technology can serve as a coping strategy to manage information effectively. Here are some ways technology-assisted solutions can be employed:

1 **Aggregation and Content Filtering:** Use content aggregation tools and news aggregators that gather information from various sources.

These tools often allow users to customize their feeds, providing a more focused and curated stream of information based on personal preferences.

2 **RSS Feeds and News Apps:** Subscribe to RSS feeds or use news apps to receive curated and personalized news updates.

These tools allow users to follow specific topics, sources, or keywords, ensuring that they stay informed about subjects of interest without being overwhelmed.

3 **AI-Powered Personal Assistants:** AI-powered personal assistants, such as Siri, Google Assistant, or Amazon Alexa, can help filter and deliver relevant information based on user preferences. Users can receive updates, summaries, and tailored content through voice commands or text queries.

4 **Customized Alerts and Notifications:** Set up customized alerts and notifications for specific topics or keywords.

This allows users to receive timely updates without continuously monitoring news feeds, social media, or other information sources.

5 **Bookmarking and Read-Later Apps:** Use bookmarking and read-later apps to save

interesting articles or content for later consumption.

This helps avoid information overload in real-time, allowing users to review content at their convenience.

6 **Data Visualization Tools:** Utilize data visualization tools to make complex information more understandable. Infographics, charts, and graphs can distill large sets of data into visually digestible formats, aiding comprehension.

7 **Educational Apps and Platforms:** Explore educational apps and platforms that provide structured and reliable content. These resources can help users deepen their understanding of specific topics

while avoiding the pitfalls of misinformation.

8 **Social Media Management Tools:** Employ social media management tools that allow users to schedule posts, track engagement, and manage multiple social media accounts from a centralized platform. This helps individuals maintain an active online presence without being overwhelmed.

9 **Collaborative Filtering:** Embrace collaborative filtering technologies that analyze user behavior and preferences to recommend relevant content.

Platforms like Netflix and Amazon use collaborative filtering to suggest movies or products based on a user's past interactions.

10 **Cybersecurity Tools:** Invest in cybersecurity tools to protect against phishing attacks, malware, and other security threats. Securing digital devices and data is essential for maintaining a safe and trustworthy online environment.

Chapter 6

The Multitasking Myth: Juggling Screens and Tasks

In the digital era, the ability to multitask has become a prized skill, often glorified as a symbol of efficiency and productivity.

This chapter delves into the multitasking myth, unraveling the truth about our capacity to juggle screens and tasks in the digital landscape and examining the consequences of attempting to do so on cognitive performance.

The Illusion of Simultaneity

The Illusion of Simultaneity refers to the perception that we can effectively multitask, engaging in multiple activities simultaneously.

Despite this common belief, research suggests that the human brain does not truly multitask in the way people often think. Instead, it rapidly switches attention between tasks, creating the illusion of simultaneity.

This phenomenon is rooted in the limitations of our cognitive processes.

Our brains have a finite capacity for attention, and attempting to focus on multiple tasks concurrently can lead to a reduction in overall performance.

When we believe we are multitasking, we are essentially engaging in rapid task-switching. Each time we shift our attention, there is a cognitive cost associated with refocusing, which can result in decreased efficiency and increased errors.

One reason for the illusion of simultaneity is that the brain can automate certain routine tasks, allowing us to perform them with minimal conscious effort.

This automation may contribute to the perception that we are simultaneously handling multiple tasks.

However, more complex tasks that require conscious thought and decision-making cannot be effectively executed in true simultaneity.

Technological advancements have also fueled the illusion of simultaneity.

The prevalence of smartphones and other devices has created an environment where individuals are constantly bombarded with information and stimuli, fostering the belief that we can efficiently process multiple streams of information simultaneously.

In reality, our brains are toggling between these streams, potentially leading to decreased overall cognitive performance.

Moreover, studies have shown that attempting to multitask can have negative effects on memory and learning.

The brain struggles to encode information effectively when attention is divided among multiple tasks.

Thus, the illusion of simultaneity may hinder our ability to retain and recall information compared to focused, single-task engagement.

Cognitive Costs of Task Switching

The cognitive costs of task switching, often referred to as "switching costs," underscore the challenges and limitations associated with shifting attention between different tasks.

When individuals engage in multitasking or frequently switch between tasks, several cognitive processes come into play, each incurring a cost that collectively affects overall cognitive performance.

1 **Time Cost:** Task switching is not instantaneous; it takes time to disengage from one task and reorient attention to another.

   This transition period, known as "switching time," adds up, leading to an overall increase in the time it takes to complete tasks. This time cost can be particularly pronounced in complex or cognitively demanding activities.

2 **Error Rate Increase:** The likelihood of making errors tends to rise when individuals switch between tasks.

   The brain needs to readjust and reestablish the context for the new task, making it more susceptible to mistakes.

This increase in error rates can be especially problematic in activities that require precision, accuracy, or careful consideration.

3 **Decreased Productivity:** Task switching can result in a reduction in overall productivity.

Constantly shifting attention between tasks may prevent individuals from reaching a state of deep focus and concentration, hindering their ability to make meaningful progress on any single task.

This decrease in productivity can be counterproductive, particularly for tasks that demand sustained attention.

4 **Increased Mental Fatigue:** The cognitive demands associated with task switching can contribute to mental fatigue.

The brain expends additional energy when repeatedly switching between tasks, leading to a sense of exhaustion.

This mental fatigue may accumulate over time, impacting overall cognitive well-being and performance.

5 **Impaired Memory Consolidation:** Effective memory consolidation requires sustained attention to encode information properly.

When attention is divided among multiple tasks, the ability to consolidate memories may be compromised.

This can result in difficulties recalling information later, hindering learning and long-term retention.

6 **Reduced Cognitive Flexibility:** Constant task switching may impede cognitive flexibility, which is the ability to adapt and switch between different mental tasks.

Prolonged exposure to switching costs might lead to a habitual pattern of fragmented attention, making it challenging for individuals to concentrate deeply on a single task when needed.

7 **Stress and Increased Cognitive Load:** The cognitive load associated with task switching can contribute to heightened stress levels.

Juggling multiple tasks simultaneously or frequently switching between them places an additional burden on cognitive resources, potentially leading to increased stress and a sense of overwhelm.

Impacts on Learning and Memory

Multitasking, often perceived as a means of enhancing productivity, has a profound negative impact on learning and memory. The human brain is not designed to efficiently handle multiple cognitive tasks simultaneously, and attempts to do so can result in diminished cognitive performance. When individuals engage in multitasking while attempting to learn or remember information, several detrimental effects become apparent.

One of the primary consequences of multitasking on learning is the phenomenon known as interference. Interference occurs when the brain struggles to process and encode information effectively due to the simultaneous engagement in multiple tasks.

The divided attention makes it challenging for the brain to focus on the relevant details of the learning material, leading to a decrease in the quality of encoding and subsequent retention.

Moreover, multitasking disrupts the consolidation of memories, a crucial process for transferring information from short-term to long-term memory.

Effective memory consolidation requires sustained attention and a focused cognitive effort. When attention is split between different tasks, the brain allocates fewer resources to the encoding and consolidation of information, resulting in a weakened memory trace.

Consequently, the ability to recall and retrieve the learned material later is compromised.

Multitasking's negative impact on learning is further exacerbated by the fact that it often involves the use of digital devices.

The constant influx of notifications, alerts, and the temptation to check emails or social media while studying creates an environment of perpetual interruption.

Each interruption requires the brain to disengage and reorient its attention, disrupting the flow of learning and impeding the formation of coherent memories.

Additionally, multitasking can lead to a shallower level of processing during learning.

When attention is divided, individuals may resort to surface-level processing rather than engaging in deep, meaningful cognitive elaboration.

Deep processing involves making connections, relating new information to existing knowledge, and critically analyzing the material—all of which are crucial for effective learning.

Shallow processing, on the other hand, results in a more superficial understanding of the material and hampers long-term retention.

In educational settings, the negative impact of multitasking on learning is a concern.

Students who attempt to multitask during lectures or while studying may experience difficulties in grasping complex concepts and retaining essential information.

The illusion of enhanced efficiency created by multitasking masks the reality of compromised cognitive processes, hindering the very learning outcomes individuals aim to achieve.

Mindful Monotasking: A Counterapproach

Mindful monotasking is a counterapproach to the prevalent multitasking culture that has become increasingly common in our fast-paced, technology-driven world.

Unlike multitasking, which involves attempting to do multiple tasks simultaneously, mindful monotasking emphasizes focusing on a single task with full attention and awareness.

This approach draws inspiration from mindfulness practices, which encourage being fully present in the moment.

Here are some key points to consider when discussing mindful monotasking:

1 **Quality over Quantity:** Mindful monotasking prioritizes the quality of work over the quantity of tasks attempted. By dedicating full attention to one task at a time, individuals can produce higher-quality results and reduce the likelihood of errors.

2 **Reduced Cognitive Load:** Multitasking often places a heavy cognitive load on the brain as it constantly switches between different tasks.

Mindful monotasking reduces cognitive load by allowing the mind to focus on a single task, leading to improved cognitive performance and reduced stress.

3 **Improved Concentration:** Monotasking promotes sustained concentration on the

task at hand. This heightened focus can lead to a deeper understanding of the subject matter and increased creativity, as the individual is not constantly shifting attention.

4 **Enhanced Productivity:** Contrary to the misconception that multitasking boosts productivity, mindful monotasking can be more efficient.

By completing one task at a time, individuals may find it easier to maintain a flow state and experience a sense of accomplishment upon task completion.

5 **Mindfulness Practices:** Mindful monotasking is closely related to mindfulness practices, such as meditation.

Incorporating mindfulness into work can lead to improved self-awareness, emotional regulation, and better decision-making.

6 **Reduced Stress and Burnout:** Constantly juggling multiple tasks can contribute to stress and burnout.

Mindful monotasking provides a reprieve from the overwhelming demands of multitasking, promoting a more sustainable and healthier work approach.

7 **Deep Work Philosophy:** Mindful monotasking aligns with the principles of deep work, as popularized by author Cal Newport.

Deep work involves focusing without distraction on cognitively demanding tasks, and it often leads to significant achievements and breakthroughs.

8 **Mindful Technology Use:** In a world dominated by technology, mindful monotasking encourages individuals to use technology more intentionally. This involves setting boundaries, minimizing distractions, and using digital tools to enhance focus rather than detract from it.

9 **Cultivating Presence:** Mindful monotasking encourages individuals to be present in the current moment, fostering a sense of mindfulness in both work and personal life. This can contribute to a more fulfilling and meaningful experience.

Chapter 7

The Filter Bubble: How Algorithms Shape Our Reality

In the digital age, algorithms wield immense power in shaping the information we encounter online.

This chapter explores the concept of the filter bubble, a phenomenon where personalized algorithms create individualized online worlds, fostering echo chambers and influencing our perceptions of reality.

The Filter Bubble Unveiled

The concept of the filter bubble, as unveiled by Eli Pariser, illuminates the unintended consequences of algorithmic personalization in our digital experiences.

At its core, the filter bubble refers to the personalized information ecosystems that algorithms create for users, tailoring content based on their past online behavior, preferences, and social interactions.

As a result, individuals find themselves enclosed in a virtual bubble, surrounded by content that aligns with their existing beliefs, interests, and viewpoints.

One significant revelation of the filter bubble is its potential impact on the diversity of information users encounter.

While the intention behind algorithmic personalization is to provide users with content they are likely to find engaging, it inadvertently limits exposure to diverse perspectives and alternative viewpoints.

Users become cocooned in a world of information that reinforces their preexisting opinions, leading to a narrowing of their informational landscape.

This narrowing effect has profound implications for democratic societies. The filter bubble can contribute to the polarization of public discourse, as individuals are shielded from dissenting opinions and differing ideologies.

The echo chamber created by algorithmic personalization can exacerbate existing divisions by deepening the rift between groups with opposing views, hindering meaningful dialogue and understanding. Additionally, the filter bubble has raised concerns about the potential for misinformation and the spread of biased content.

When users are primarily exposed to information that aligns with their existing beliefs, they may be less equipped to critically evaluate the accuracy and credibility of the content they encounter.

This can create a fertile ground for the dissemination of misinformation, as users may unknowingly accept and share content that reinforces their worldview, regardless of its veracity.

Echo Chambers: Reinforcing Beliefs and Biases

Echo chambers represent virtual spaces where individuals are surrounded by like-minded opinions and perspectives, creating a reinforcing loop that solidifies their existing beliefs and biases.

These chambers are often a consequence of social and digital algorithms that tailor content to align with users' preferences, fostering an environment where individuals are consistently exposed to information that mirrors their own views.

The consequence of this phenomenon is the entrenchment of existing beliefs, as users are seldom confronted with dissenting opinions or alternative perspectives.

Within echo chambers, the reinforcement of beliefs and biases occurs through a self-perpetuating cycle. Users are exposed to content that resonates with their preexisting views, leading to increased engagement and interaction with such content.

Algorithms, in turn, interpret this engagement as a signal of user preference, further fine-tuning the content to cater to the user's specific worldview.

This closed-loop system inadvertently isolates individuals from diverse perspectives, contributing to the solidification of their existing beliefs.

Political Implications: Polarization and Fragmentation

The filter bubble, driven by algorithmic personalization, has profound political implications, notably in the form of polarization and fragmentation within societies.

As individuals are exposed to content that aligns with their existing beliefs and preferences, the filter bubble contributes to the deepening of ideological divisions.

This polarization occurs as users are insulated from diverse perspectives, hindering the formation of a shared understanding and common ground among citizens.

In the realm of politics, the filter bubble intensifies existing partisan divides. Users within a filter bubble are more likely to encounter information that reinforces their political inclinations and less likely to be exposed to opposing viewpoints.

This reinforcement of existing beliefs can lead to a hardening of political attitudes, making it challenging for individuals to engage in constructive dialogue with those who hold differing opinions.

The filter bubble, therefore, becomes a catalyst for the formation of echo chambers where like-minded individuals strengthen each other's convictions while remaining isolated from alternative political ideologies.

The fragmentation of information within filter bubbles also has implications for the democratic process. In a fragmented information landscape, citizens may lack a comprehensive understanding of diverse perspectives on political issues.

This limited exposure can impede informed decision-making, as voters may be swayed by a narrow range of viewpoints without a holistic understanding of the complex issues at hand.

Consequently, the filter bubble contributes to a fragmented political discourse, potentially eroding the foundation of a well-informed and participatory democracy. Furthermore, the filter bubble can be exploited by political actors seeking to manipulate public opinion.

In a polarized and fragmented environment, disinformation and misleading narratives can spread more easily, taking advantage of the lack of exposure to diverse sources that might provide a more accurate and nuanced understanding of political events.

The targeted nature of filter bubbles makes certain segments of the population more susceptible to manipulation, as tailored content can reinforce preexisting biases and shape perceptions.

Escaping the Bubble: Strategies for Digital Literacy

Escaping the filter bubble and promoting digital literacy are crucial endeavors in an age where personalized algorithms shape our online experiences. Digital literacy involves the ability to critically evaluate, navigate, and interact with digital information.

Here are strategies for individuals to enhance their digital literacy and break free from the confines of the filter bubble:

1 **Diversify Your Sources:** Actively seek out information from a variety of sources,

including those with differing perspectives.

Following a diverse range of news outlets, opinion pieces, and social media accounts can provide a more balanced and comprehensive understanding of issues.

2 **Check and Challenge Your Biases:** Be aware of your own biases and regularly challenge them. Actively seek information that challenges your existing beliefs to foster a more nuanced and well-rounded perspective. This can help break the reinforcement cycle of the filter bubble.

3 **Learn About Algorithms:** Gain a basic understanding of how algorithms work,

particularly those employed by social media platforms.

Recognize that these algorithms aim to keep users engaged, often by showing content similar to what they have previously engaged with, contributing to the filter bubble.

Being aware of these mechanisms is the first step to navigating them effectively.

4 **Use Privacy Settings Wisely:** Understand and manage your privacy settings on digital platforms.

Adjusting these settings can influence the type of content and advertisements you are exposed to. Take control of your online environment to limit the extent of personalization.

5 **Fact-Checking Skills:** Develop strong fact-checking skills to discern credible information from misinformation.

Cross-reference information from multiple sources and consult fact-checking websites to verify the accuracy of claims, especially before sharing information.

6 **Engage in Civil Discourse:** Foster open and respectful conversations with individuals holding different viewpoints. Engaging in civil discourse helps break down echo chambers by exposing you to alternative perspectives and challenging your own assumptions.

7 **Be Mindful of Clickbait:** Be cautious of sensationalized headlines or clickbait.

Clicking on misleading or emotionally charged content can contribute to the reinforcement of the filter bubble. Evaluate the credibility of information before engaging with it.

8 **Educational Initiatives:** Support and participate in educational initiatives that promote digital literacy.

These initiatives can include workshops, online courses, or community programs aimed at enhancing critical thinking skills in the digital age.

9 **Limit Screen Time:** While online, be mindful of the time spent on digital platforms.

Excessive screen time can contribute to the intensification of the filter bubble.

Balancing online and offline activities helps maintain a broader perspective.

10 **Regularly Review and Refresh:** Periodically review your social media feeds, subscriptions, and news sources. Refreshing your digital environment by adding or removing sources ensures that you actively curate a diverse and informative online experience.

Chapter 8

The Virtual Reality Shift: Exploring Immersive Experiences

As technology advances, virtual reality (VR) has emerged as a transformative force, reshaping how we perceive and interact with the world.

This chapter delves into the profound impact of virtual reality on our cognition, examining the ways in which immersive experiences alter our perception of reality and influence cognitive processes.

The Evolution of Virtual Reality

The evolution of virtual reality (VR) has been a fascinating journey, marked by significant technological advancements and a growing integration into various aspects of our lives. Initially conceptualized in the mid-20th century, the idea of immersive, computer-generated environments gained traction as computing power increased.

The first primitive VR systems emerged in the late 1960s and early 1970s, often characterized by rudimentary graphics and limited interactivity.

However, these early experiments laid the groundwork for the development of more sophisticated VR technologies.

The 1990s witnessed a surge in interest and investment in VR, with the emergence of consumer-oriented devices like the Virtual Boy by Nintendo and VR arcade games.

Despite initial enthusiasm, technological constraints, such as low display resolutions and cumbersome hardware, hindered widespread adoption.

The early 2000s saw a decline in VR popularity as expectations outpaced available technology.

A significant turning point came in the 2010s when advancements in computing power, graphics processing, and motion tracking reignited interest in VR.

The release of devices like the Oculus Rift, HTC Vive, and PlayStation VR marked a new era, offering more immersive experiences with higher fidelity graphics and improved tracking capabilities.

These developments sparked a renaissance in VR applications, extending beyond gaming to fields like education, healthcare, and corporate training.

Mobile VR further democratized access to virtual experiences by leveraging the processing power of smartphones.

Devices like the Google Cardboard and Samsung Gear VR provided affordable entry points for users to explore VR content.

However, these systems still faced limitations in terms of graphical quality and interaction capabilities.

In recent years, standalone VR devices, have taken center stage, eliminating the need for tethered connections to computers or consoles.

These standalone systems offer an unprecedented level of freedom, allowing users to move within a virtual space without external constraints.

Additionally, the integration of hand tracking, haptic feedback, and other sensory elements has enhanced the sense of presence in virtual environments.

The evolution of VR is not only about hardware but also the development of a robust ecosystem of software and content.

VR applications now extend beyond entertainment to include virtual tourism, architectural visualization, therapy, and collaborative workspaces.

The metaverse, a collective virtual shared space, is increasingly becoming a topic of discussion, hinting at a future where VR plays a central role in how we socialize, work, and interact with digital content.

Looking ahead, ongoing research and development continue to push the boundaries of VR technology.

Advancements in areas like artificial intelligence, 5G connectivity, and more immersive display technologies promise to further enhance the capabilities of virtual reality.

As VR becomes more integrated into our daily lives, the evolution of this technology is poised to redefine the way we perceive and interact with the digital and physical worlds.

Perception Redefined: The Illusion of Presence

Perception in virtual reality (VR) represents a paradigm shift in how individuals engage with digital environments, and one of its hallmark features is the illusion of presence. Presence, in the context of VR, refers to the feeling of being physically and mentally situated in a computer-generated space as if it were real.

This psychological phenomenon is a cornerstone of immersive experiences and distinguishes VR from traditional forms of media.

The illusion of presence is achieved through a combination of advanced technologies that stimulate multiple sensory channels.

Visual stimuli, delivered through high-resolution displays and sophisticated graphics, play a pivotal role.

The more realistic and detailed the virtual environment appears, the stronger the sense of presence becomes.

Additionally, spatial audio and three-dimensional sound contribute to a more immersive experience, enhancing the feeling of being present within the digital space.

One crucial aspect of presence is the integration of head tracking and motion controllers.

As users move their heads or interact with the virtual world through gestures, the system responds in real-time, reinforcing the illusion that they exist within the created environment.

This dynamic interaction creates a profound connection between the user and the digital space, fostering a sense of agency and immersion.

Psychological factors also contribute significantly to the illusion of presence. Users often report a suspension of disbelief, willingly accepting the artificial environment as real, despite a conscious awareness of its digital nature.

The brain, influenced by sensory input and cognitive processes, adapts to the virtual context, blurring the lines between the physical and virtual realms.

Presence has transformative implications across various fields. In gaming, it elevates the level of engagement, making experiences more emotionally resonant and memorable.

In education, virtual classrooms offer students the opportunity to feel present in historical events or far-off locations, enhancing learning outcomes.

In healthcare, VR simulations enable medical professionals to practice procedures in a virtual environment, refining their skills with a heightened sense of realism.

However, the illusion of presence is a delicate construct, and disruptions can lead to a phenomenon known as "cybersickness." Issues such as lag in motion tracking or inconsistencies between visual and vestibular cues can break the illusion, causing discomfort or nausea.

Achieving a seamless sense of presence requires not only cutting-edge hardware but also careful attention to design principles that align with the perceptual expectations of the human brain.

As technology continues to advance, pushing the boundaries of visual fidelity, interactivity, and sensory feedback, the illusion of presence in virtual reality is likely to become even more convincing.

The ongoing exploration of haptic feedback, olfactory stimulation, and advancements in artificial intelligence may further deepen the immersive qualities of VR, redefining our understanding of perception and opening up new frontiers in the intersection of the digital and physical worlds.

Cognitive Impact of Virtual Reality

Virtual Reality (VR) has the potential to significantly impact cognitive processes and functions, influencing various aspects of perception, memory, learning, and behavior. Here are some key ways in which VR can affect cognition:

Enhanced Learning and Training

1 **Immersive Learning Environments:** VR provides an immersive and interactive learning experience, allowing users to engage with content in a three-dimensional space. This can enhance learning retention and understanding.

2 **Hands-On Training:** VR simulations enable users to practice skills in a realistic and safe environment. This is particularly beneficial in fields such as medicine, aviation, and military training.

Spatial Cognition

1 **Spatial Awareness:** VR can enhance spatial awareness by providing users with

a sense of depth and dimension. This can be especially useful in fields like architecture, where professionals can explore virtual spaces before they are constructed.

2 **Navigation Skills:** VR experiences can improve spatial navigation skills as users interact with virtual environments, contributing to better wayfinding abilities.

Memory and Recall

3 **Memory Formation:** VR experiences can create more memorable events, as the brain tends to better retain information associated with emotional or spatial contexts. This can be leveraged for

educational purposes and in therapeutic interventions.

4 **Contextual Learning:** By embedding information within a spatial context, VR can enhance contextual learning, where users remember information better when it is presented in a relevant environment.

Emotional Impact

5 **Emotional Engagement:** VR has the ability to evoke strong emotional responses due to its immersive nature. This emotional engagement can impact memory and learning, making experiences more impactful and memorable.

6 **Therapeutic Applications:** VR is used in therapeutic interventions for conditions like phobias, PTSD, and anxiety disorders. Exposure therapy in a controlled virtual environment can help individuals confront and manage their fears.

Cognitive Load and Attention

7 **Reduced Cognitive Load:** VR can provide a more intuitive and natural interface, reducing the cognitive load associated with traditional interfaces. This is particularly relevant in tasks that require a high level of attention and multitasking.

8 **Selective Attention:** VR experiences can guide users' attention more effectively by controlling the visual and auditory stimuli

in the virtual environment.

Social Cognition

9 **Social Interaction:** VR allows for social interactions in virtual spaces, contributing to the study of social cognition. It can be used to simulate social scenarios for research, training, or therapeutic purposes.

Neuroplasticity and Rehabilitation

10 **Neurological Rehabilitation:** VR is being explored as a tool for neurorehabilitation, helping individuals recover from neurological injuries or conditions by promoting neuroplasticity through engaging and repetitive tasks.

While VR presents exciting opportunities for cognitive enhancement, it's important to consider ethical concerns, potential negative effects (such as motion sickness), and the need for further research to fully understand the long-term cognitive impact of prolonged VR use.

Ethical Considerations and Challenges

The rapid development and widespread adoption of Virtual Reality (VR) technologies bring about various ethical considerations and challenges. Here are some key issues that need careful consideration:

Privacy Concerns

1 **Data Collection and Storage:** VR experiences often involve the collection of user data, including movement patterns, interactions, and even physiological responses. Ensuring the responsible collection and storage of this data to protect users' privacy is crucial.

2 **Informed Consent:** Users should be fully informed about the data being collected and how it will be used. Obtaining informed consent becomes challenging when users may not fully understand the potential implications of their virtual experiences.

Content and User Safety

3 **Inappropriate Content:** VR content can range from educational to entertainment, but there's a risk of inappropriate or harmful content. Ensuring content moderation and age-appropriate restrictions is important.

4 **Psychological Impact:** Immersive experiences can have a profound psychological impact. Designers and developers must consider the potential for triggering anxiety, stress, or other negative emotions and take steps to mitigate these effects.

Digital Addiction and Behavioral Impact

5 **Overuse and Addiction:** Extended use of VR may lead to digital addiction and impact users' daily lives negatively. Developers should encourage responsible usage and create mechanisms to prevent excessive immersion.

6 **Behavioral Changes:** VR can influence behavior by creating experiences that might not be feasible or acceptable in the physical world. Developers should consider the ethical implications of encouraging certain behaviors within virtual spaces.

Accessibility and Inclusivity

7 **Physical Accessibility:** VR systems might not be easily accessible for individuals with physical disabilities. Designing for inclusivity is essential to ensure that everyone can benefit from VR experiences.

8 **Economic Disparities:** VR technology can be expensive, creating a digital divide where only certain socioeconomic groups can access its benefits. Addressing these disparities is crucial to prevent further inequality.

Cybersecurity and Hacking

9 **Data Security:** As with any digital technology, VR is susceptible to

cybersecurity threats. Protecting user data and preventing unauthorized access is essential to maintain trust in VR systems.

10 **Identity Theft:** VR interactions may involve personal avatars and profiles, raising the risk of identity theft within virtual spaces. Ensuring robust authentication mechanisms is vital.

Informed Design and User Empowerment

11 **Transparency in Design:** Developers should be transparent about how VR experiences are designed and how user data is used. Providing users with control over their settings and preferences

contributes to ethical design.

12 **Empowering Users:** Educating users about the potential impact of VR on their cognition, emotions, and behaviors empowers them to make informed decisions about their virtual experiences.

Long-term Physical Effects:

Prolonged use of VR may lead to physical discomfort, eye strain, and motion sickness. Developers should prioritize user health and well-being by implementing features that reduce potential adverse effects.

Social and Ethical Norms:

VR can challenge traditional social norms as users interact in virtual environments. Establishing ethical guidelines for behavior within these spaces is essential to prevent harassment and abuse.

Global and Cultural Sensitivity

VR content should be mindful of cultural sensitivities to avoid appropriation or misrepresentation. Developers should consider the diverse backgrounds and beliefs of users worldwide.

The Future of Immersive Experiences

The future of immersive experiences with virtual reality (VR) holds tremendous promise, as technological advancements continue to push the boundaries of what is possible.

As hardware becomes more sophisticated and affordable, VR is expected to play an increasingly integral role in various sectors, ranging from entertainment and education to healthcare and beyond.

In the realm of entertainment, the future of VR promises to revolutionize how we consume media. Virtual reality can transport users into entirely new worlds, offering unparalleled levels of immersion in gaming, cinema, and interactive storytelling.

As content creators harness the full potential of VR, audiences can anticipate more engaging and lifelike experiences that blur the lines between reality and the virtual realm.

Education stands to benefit significantly from the evolution of VR. Immersive learning environments can provide students with hands-on experiences that were previously impossible, such as virtual field trips, interactive simulations, and three-dimensional models.

This not only enhances the learning process but also accommodates various learning styles, making education more accessible and inclusive.

In healthcare, VR is poised to make substantial contributions to both diagnostics and treatment.

Medical professionals can use VR simulations for surgical training, allowing them to practice procedures in a risk-free environment.

Additionally, VR therapy has shown promise in treating conditions such as PTSD and phobias, providing patients with a controlled and customizable therapeutic experience.

The workplace is another domain where the future of immersive experiences is taking shape.

VR technologies enable remote collaboration in virtual offices, transcending geographical constraints and fostering more dynamic and interactive team interactions.

Training programs can leverage VR for realistic and hands-on simulations, particularly in industries that require specialized skills or hazardous conditions.

As the future unfolds, advancements in augmented reality (AR) are likely to complement the immersive experiences offered by VR.

The combination of AR and VR, known as mixed reality, has the potential to create seamless, context-aware experiences that integrate virtual elements into the physical world.

This convergence could lead to transformative changes in how we perceive and interact with our surroundings.

However, alongside these exciting prospects, ethical considerations and potential challenges must be carefully navigated.

Privacy concerns, content moderation, and the societal impact of extended VR use warrant ongoing attention.

Striking a balance between innovation and ethical responsibility will be crucial in shaping a future where immersive experiences enhance our lives while respecting fundamental values and principles.

Chapter 9

Mindful Tech: Balancing Connectivity and Mental Well-being

In the era of constant connectivity, the relationship between technology use and mental well-being has become increasingly intricate.

This chapter explores the significance of cultivating a mindful approach to technology use, emphasizing the pivotal role it plays in maintaining mental health amid the digital landscape.

Mindful Tech: A Holistic Approach

"Mindful Tech: A Holistic Approach" refers to an approach that integrates technology with mindfulness practices to enhance well-being and promote a healthier relationship with technology.

In today's fast-paced digital world, where technology is deeply integrated into our daily lives, there is a growing awareness of the need for a more balanced and mindful use of technology to mitigate its potential negative impacts on mental health, focus, and overall well-being.

Here are some key aspects of a mindful tech approach:

1 **Awareness and Intention:** Mindful tech encourages users to be aware of their

technology use and to approach it with intention.

This involves being conscious of when, why, and how we use technology and whether it aligns with our goals and values.

2 **Digital Detox:** Mindful tech involves periodic breaks or digital detoxes to disconnect from screens and constant connectivity.

This allows individuals to recharge, reflect, and engage in activities that promote well-being without the distractions of technology.

3 **Mindful Design:** Designing technology with mindfulness in mind involves creating user interfaces and experiences

that are intuitive, less distracting, and support focused attention.

This might include features that encourage breaks, limit notifications, or provide user-friendly interfaces.

4 **Mindfulness Apps and Tools:** There is a growing market for apps and tools that promote mindfulness, meditation, and stress reduction.

These apps often leverage technology to provide guided meditation, breathing exercises, and other mindfulness practices, making them easily accessible to users.

5 **Balance and Moderation:** Mindful tech advocates for a balanced and moderate use of technology.

It emphasizes the importance of finding a healthy equilibrium between the benefits of technology and the need for real-world experiences, face-to-face interactions, and other non-digital activities.

6 **Education and Training:** Promoting a mindful tech approach involves educating individuals about the potential impact of technology on their well-being and providing training on how to use technology mindfully.

This can be integrated into educational curricula, workplace wellness programs, and community initiatives.

7 **Reflection and Self-Awareness:** Mindful tech encourages individuals to reflect on

their technology use and its effects on their lives.

This self-awareness can lead to informed choices and adjustments in behavior to create a healthier relationship with technology.

8 **Corporate Responsibility:** Companies are increasingly recognizing their role in promoting mindful tech practices.

This involves designing products and services that prioritize user well-being, as well as providing tools and resources to help users maintain a healthy relationship with technology.

Building a Mindful Tech Culture

Building a mindful tech culture involves fostering an environment within organizations that encourages employees to develop a balanced and conscious relationship with technology.

Such a culture recognizes the importance of well-being, mindfulness, and a healthy work-life-tech balance. Here are key aspects to consider when building a mindful tech culture:

1 **Leadership and Role Modeling:** Leadership plays a crucial role in shaping organizational culture. Executives and managers should actively promote and model mindful tech practices.

When leaders prioritize well-being and emphasize the importance of taking breaks, it sets a positive example for the entire workforce.

2 **Education and Training:** Providing education and training on mindful tech practices is essential.

This can include workshops, seminars, or online resources that educate employees about the impact of technology on well-being and teach practical mindfulness techniques.

Ensuring that employees are informed empowers them to make conscious choices regarding their technology use.

3 **Clear Communication:** Establish open communication about the expectations

regarding technology use within the organization.

Clearly communicate policies on after-hours communication, response time expectations, and the importance of taking breaks. Transparency fosters understanding and reduces stress associated with uncertainty.

4 **Flexible Work Arrangements:** Consider implementing flexible work arrangements that acknowledge and accommodate employees' diverse needs. This might include options for remote work, flexible hours, or compressed workweeks. Allowing flexibility recognizes that individuals have different preferences and rhythms for work.

5 **Designing Mindful Workspaces:** Physical and digital workspaces can be designed to promote mindfulness.

This includes creating comfortable and ergonomic physical environments as well as designing digital interfaces that minimize distraction and support focused work.

Incorporating elements of nature, providing quiet spaces, and offering ergonomic furniture contribute to a mindful work environment.

6 **Encouraging Breaks and Downtime:** Encourage employees to take regular breaks and vacations. Emphasize the importance of stepping away from screens and work-related tasks to

recharge.

Some organizations even promote the use of mindfulness apps or offer meditation rooms to facilitate relaxation and stress reduction.

7 **Technology Etiquette:** Establish guidelines for respectful and mindful technology use, especially in meetings and collaborative settings.

Encourage employees to be present and fully engaged during discussions, minimizing distractions from devices.

Establishing technology etiquette helps create a more focused and respectful work environment.

8 **Recognition of Overwork:** Acknowledge and address the issue of overwork.

Recognize that constantly being connected and working long hours can lead to burnout.

Encourage employees to set boundaries and prioritize self-care. Celebrate accomplishments but also recognize the importance of a sustainable pace.

9 **Feedback and Iteration:** Foster a culture of continuous improvement. Seek feedback from employees regarding the effectiveness of mindful tech initiatives and be willing to iterate on strategies based on this feedback.

This demonstrates a commitment to adapting to the evolving needs and expectations of the workforce.

10 **Community and Support:** Foster a sense of community and support among employees. This can involve creating wellness programs, organizing social events, or establishing support networks within the organization.

A supportive community reinforces the importance of well-being and encourages employees to prioritize self-care.

Chapter 10

Digital Literacy: Navigating the Information Landscape

In an era dominated by digital information, cultivating digital literacy is paramount for individuals to navigate the vast and often complex landscape of online content.

This chapter explores the significance of digital literacy, offering insights and strategies to empower readers with the skills needed to critically evaluate and engage with information in the digital age.

The Information Explosion

The information explosion characterizes the unprecedented growth and proliferation of data and knowledge in the modern era, primarily fueled by advancements in technology and digital communication.

The advent of the internet, coupled with the rapid development of information and communication technologies, has led to an exponential increase in the volume, velocity, and variety of data available to individuals and organizations.

This explosion has profound implications for various facets of society, including communication, education, business, and culture.

One significant aspect of the information explosion is the democratization of knowledge. The internet has become a vast repository of information, making it accessible to people around the globe.

This democratization has facilitated the sharing of ideas, the dissemination of information, and the democratization of education.

However, it also brings challenges related to information quality, credibility, and the ability to navigate the overwhelming abundance of data.

In the realm of communication, the information explosion has transformed how people connect and share ideas. Social media platforms, blogs, podcasts, and other online channels allow individuals to express themselves and share information on a global scale.

This democratization of communication empowers voices that may have been marginalized in traditional media but also raises concerns about misinformation, echo chambers, and the polarization of public discourse.

In business, the information explosion has led to the rise of big data and analytics. Organizations can harness vast amounts of data to make informed decisions, optimize processes, and gain insights into consumer behavior.

However, the challenge lies in managing, analyzing, and extracting meaningful insights from this abundance of information.

Additionally, issues related to data privacy, security, and ethical considerations become prominent in the context of the information explosion.

Education has also undergone a significant transformation due to the information explosion. Access to online resources, e-learning platforms, and open educational materials has expanded educational opportunities globally.

However, the sheer volume of available information poses challenges for educators and learners alike.

Developing critical thinking skills and the ability to discern reliable sources become crucial in navigating the vast landscape of information.

Culturally, the information explosion has influenced how people consume media and entertainment. Streaming services, digital publications, and online content platforms offer a wide array of choices to audiences. While this provides diverse options for entertainment and information consumption, it also raises questions about the impact on traditional media industries and the potential for information overload.

Defining Digital Literacy

Digital literacy encompasses a range of skills and competencies essential for navigating the complex and dynamic digital landscape.

These pillars serve as the foundation for acquiring, evaluating, and utilizing information in the digital age.

1 **Information Literacy:** Information literacy is a cornerstone of digital literacy. It involves the ability to locate, evaluate, and use information critically and ethically.

    This pillar empowers individuals to discern credible sources, distinguish between reliable and misleading information, and navigate vast digital repositories effectively.

2 **Media Literacy:** Media literacy is crucial for understanding and analyzing various forms of media, including text, images,

audio, and video.

This pillar enables individuals to interpret media messages, identify bias, and critically assess the impact of media on society. In the digital era, media literacy is essential for navigating the diverse and sometimes overwhelming media landscape.

3 **Communication and Collaboration:** Digital literacy includes the ability to communicate effectively and collaborate in digital environments.

This pillar encompasses skills such as online etiquette, effective use of communication tools, and collaboration through digital platforms.

As digital communication becomes integral to personal and professional interactions, these skills are vital for meaningful engagement.

4 **Critical Thinking:** Critical thinking is a foundational pillar that underlies many aspects of digital literacy. It involves the ability to analyze, synthesize, and evaluate information and arguments.

In the digital context, critical thinking helps individuals navigate the abundance of information, question assumptions, and make informed decisions in various online environments.

5 **Digital Security and Privacy:** As individuals engage with digital platforms, understanding digital security and privacy

becomes paramount.

This pillar involves knowledge of how to protect personal information, recognize and respond to online threats, and use digital tools securely.

Digital security and privacy literacy contribute to safe and responsible online behavior.

6 **Technological Literacy:** Technological literacy involves understanding the basic principles of technology and the ability to use digital tools effectively.

This pillar includes skills such as proficiency in using software applications, adapting to new technologies, and troubleshooting common technical issues.

Technological literacy empowers individuals to navigate and leverage digital tools for personal and professional growth.

7 **Ethical Considerations:** Ethical considerations are a crucial aspect of digital literacy, encompassing the understanding of digital ethics, online etiquette, and responsible digital citizenship.

This pillar involves recognizing the impact of digital actions on oneself and others, respecting intellectual property rights, and promoting positive online behavior.

8 **Adaptability and Lifelong Learning:** Digital literacy is not static; it requires an adaptive mindset and a commitment to

lifelong learning.

This pillar involves staying informed about emerging technologies, being open to acquiring new digital skills, and continuously updating one's knowledge to navigate evolving digital landscapes.

Strategies for Developing Digital Literacy

1. **Continuous Learning:** Stay informed about evolving digital landscapes, new technologies, and emerging online trends. Engage in lifelong learning to adapt and enhance digital literacy skills.

2. **Fact-Checking:** Develop the habit of fact-checking information encountered online. Verify information through reputable

sources before accepting and sharing it with others.

3. Diverse Source Consumption: Consume information from a variety of sources to gain diverse perspectives. Avoid relying solely on one outlet or viewpoint to cultivate a well-rounded understanding of a topic.

4. Critical Evaluation Tools: Familiarize yourself with tools and techniques for critical evaluation. This includes understanding website credibility, fact-checking websites, and utilizing browser extensions that identify potentially unreliable sources.

Strategies for Fostering Digital Literacy Skill

Nurturing digital literacy is vital in the swiftly evolving technological landscape of today, and there are specific actions we should take to promote these skills. Here are several strategies for cultivating digital literacy skills:

1 **Formal Education Integration:** Integrate digital literacy into formal education curricula at all levels.

Develop comprehensive programs that cover information literacy, media literacy, critical thinking, and ethical considerations.

Encourage hands-on experiences with digital tools to enhance practical skills.

2 **Teacher Training:** Provide educators with training on digital literacy so that they can effectively teach and model these skills to students.

Continuous professional development ensures that educators stay abreast of evolving technologies and can guide students in navigating the digital landscape responsibly.

3 **Incorporate Digital Tools in Learning:** Integrate digital tools and resources into classroom activities.

This could involve using educational apps, online research, collaborative platforms, and multimedia creation tools. Hands-on experience with these tools enhances digital literacy skills.

4 **Project-Based Learning:** Implement project-based learning approaches that require students to research, analyze, and present information using digital tools.

This fosters critical thinking, problem-solving, and collaboration skills while providing practical experience with technology.

5 **Interactive Workshops and Training Sessions:** Conduct interactive workshops and training sessions for students, teachers, and even parents.

Cover topics such as online safety, digital communication, evaluating information sources, and ethical considerations. Workshops can be tailored to specific age groups and digital literacy levels.

6 **Community Outreach Programs:** Extend digital literacy initiatives to the broader community.

This could involve workshops, seminars, or online resources aimed at adults, seniors, and other community members.

Addressing digital literacy across generations contributes to a more digitally inclusive society.

7 **Online Courses and MOOCs:** Leverage online courses and Massive Open Online Courses (MOOCs) to provide accessible and flexible digital literacy training.

Platforms like Coursera, edX, and Khan Academy offer courses covering various aspects of digital literacy.

8 **Partnerships with Tech Industry:** Collaborate with technology companies to provide resources, expertise, and mentorship programs.

Tech industry partnerships can offer insights into current trends, emerging technologies, and real-world applications of digital literacy skills.

9 **Digital Literacy Certification Programs:** Develop and promote digital literacy certification programs. These programs can serve as formal recognition of an individual's proficiency in digital literacy, making them valuable in academic and professional settings.

10 **Parental Engagement Programs:** Educate parents on the importance of digital

literacy and provide resources to support their children's digital learning.

Parental involvement is crucial for reinforcing digital literacy skills at home and promoting safe online behavior.

11 **Gamified Learning Platforms:** Explore gamified learning platforms that engage users through interactive and entertaining experiences.

Gamification can make learning digital literacy more enjoyable and effective, especially for younger audiences.

12 **Continuous Learning Platforms for Educators:** Establish platforms or networks that facilitate continuous learning for educators.

This can include forums, webinars, and collaborative spaces where educators can share best practices, discuss challenges, and stay informed about the latest developments in digital literacy.

Chapter 11

The Future Mind: Adapting to Technological Advancements

As technology advances at an unprecedented pace, the future promises transformative developments that will reshape the way we think, learn, and interact.

This chapter explores potential future advancements in technology and their profound implications for the evolution of our cognitive processes and the very nature of the human mind.

The Acceleration of Technological Progress

The trajectory of technological advancement paints a compelling picture of a future marked by innovations that extend far beyond our current imagination, particularly in the realm of cognition.

As we delve into the possibilities on the horizon, emerging technologies hold the promise of transforming the landscape of how we perceive, understand, and enhance human cognitive abilities.

One notable area of exploration is the convergence of neuroscience and technology.

Advancements in brain-computer interfaces (BCIs) have the potential to revolutionize the way we interact with the digital world. From controlling devices with our thoughts to augmenting cognitive functions, BCIs could open new frontiers for individuals with disabilities and unlock previously unimaginable capabilities for the broader population.

The seamless integration of the human mind with external devices may redefine the boundaries of cognition, allowing for enhanced memory, faster information processing, and even novel forms of communication.

Artificial intelligence (AI) stands as a central player in shaping the future landscape of cognition.

Machine learning algorithms, neural networks, and deep learning techniques continue to evolve, offering unprecedented capabilities in data analysis and pattern recognition.

These advancements not only contribute to the development of more intelligent systems but also pave the way for AI-assisted cognition.

From personalized learning experiences to adaptive decision-making support, AI has the potential to augment and amplify human cognitive abilities, leading to a synergistic partnership between humans and machines.

Virtual and augmented reality technologies are poised to redefine the way we perceive and interact with information.

As these technologies advance, they will likely immerse users in virtual environments that simulate real-world scenarios, creating opportunities for experiential learning and enhanced cognitive engagement.

Moreover, augmented reality could overlay digital information onto our physical surroundings, offering a seamless integration of the digital and physical realms and transforming how we access and process information in our daily lives.

Quantum computing represents a frontier that holds immense promise for the future of cognition.

Unlike classical computers, quantum computers leverage the principles of quantum mechanics to perform computations at speeds inconceivable with current technology.

The potential applications range from solving complex optimization problems to simulating molecular interactions, presenting a paradigm shift in our ability to understand and manipulate information at a fundamental level.

Quantum computing could unlock new possibilities in fields such as drug discovery, materials science, and artificial intelligence.

However, as we explore the exciting prospects of technological advancements in cognition, ethical considerations become paramount.

Questions surrounding privacy, consent, and the responsible use of these technologies must be addressed.

Striking a balance between innovation and ethical considerations will be crucial in ensuring that the future landscape of cognition is shaped with a focus on societal well-being and inclusivity.

Brain-Computer Interfaces: Merging Mind and Machine

Brain-Computer Interfaces (BCIs) represent a cutting-edge field of technological innovation that aims to bridge the gap between the human brain and machines.

This merging of mind and machine holds tremendous potential to revolutionize the way we interact with technology, opening new avenues for communication, control, and even enhancement of cognitive capabilities.

BCIs operate by translating neural signals from the brain into actionable commands for external devices, creating a direct link between the human brain and computers.

One of the primary applications of BCIs is in the realm of assistive technology. For individuals with paralysis or severe motor impairments, BCIs offer a means to regain control and independence.

By capturing brain signals associated with intention or movement, these interfaces enable users to manipulate prosthetic limbs, control wheelchairs, or even communicate through typing or speech synthesis.

BCIs have the potential to significantly enhance the quality of life for people with disabilities by restoring a degree of autonomy that was previously unattainable.

Beyond assistive applications, BCIs are paving the way for novel human-computer interactions. Experimental research explores the use of BCIs in gaming, virtual reality, and other immersive experiences.

By interpreting users' neural signals, BCIs can provide a more seamless and intuitive interface, allowing individuals to control digital environments with their thoughts.

This not only holds entertainment value but also has implications for training, education, and simulation scenarios where natural and direct interaction is crucial.

In the field of cognitive enhancement, BCIs are being explored as a means to augment human capabilities.

Research efforts are focused on developing BCIs that can enhance memory, attention, and decision-making processes.

While these applications are in the early stages of development, they raise ethical considerations regarding the potential for creating disparities in cognitive abilities and the need for responsible and equitable deployment of such technologies.

The future of BCIs holds the promise of unlocking new frontiers in understanding the intricacies of the human brain.

Advances in neuroscientific research, coupled with improvements in sensor technology and data processing, contribute to the refinement of BCIs.

Researchers are exploring the development of non-invasive BCIs that rely on wearable sensors, reducing the need for surgical procedures.

Additionally, innovations in materials science and neuroengineering aim to create more biocompatible and durable interfaces.

However, the widespread adoption of BCIs raises ethical and privacy concerns. Issues related to consent, data security, and the potential misuse of neural information must be carefully addressed.

As BCIs become more sophisticated, ensuring that ethical frameworks and regulations keep pace with technological advancements becomes imperative to safeguard individual autonomy and privacy.

Artificial Intelligence and Cognitive Enhancement

Artificial Intelligence (AI) and cognitive enhancement are two intertwined domains that hold significant implications for the future of human capabilities.

AI, characterized by machine learning algorithms and advanced computational power, has the potential to augment and amplify human cognitive functions.

While these advancements offer numerous opportunities, they also raise ethical questions and considerations regarding the responsible use of technology to enhance cognitive abilities.

AI plays a pivotal role in cognitive enhancement by providing tools and systems that complement and extend human intelligence.

Smart assistants, language translation services, and recommendation algorithms are everyday examples of AI enhancing our cognitive capacities.

These applications leverage machine learning to analyze vast datasets, recognize patterns, and generate insights, ultimately facilitating more efficient decision-making and problem-solving for individuals and organizations.

In the realm of healthcare, AI contributes to cognitive enhancement through diagnostic and predictive capabilities.

Machine learning algorithms analyze medical data, identify patterns in patient records, and assist healthcare professionals in making more accurate diagnoses and treatment plans.

AI-driven tools can significantly enhance the cognitive abilities of medical practitioners, leading to improved patient outcomes and more personalized healthcare.

However, the convergence of AI and cognitive enhancement also poses ethical challenges. Questions arise about the potential for technology-driven disparities in cognitive abilities and access to enhancement tools.

Issues related to privacy, consent, and the responsible use of AI in influencing human cognition warrant careful consideration.

Ethical frameworks must be established to ensure that cognitive enhancement technologies are deployed in a manner that upholds individual autonomy, promotes equity, and mitigates potential risks.

Cognitive enhancement extends beyond AI to include direct interventions aimed at improving human cognitive abilities.

Neuroenhancement techniques, such as brain stimulation and pharmaceutical interventions, raise ethical questions regarding safety, long-term effects, and societal implications.

As these technologies advance, it becomes essential to strike a balance between the potential benefits of cognitive enhancement and the need to address ethical concerns, ensuring that the pursuit of enhancement aligns with human values and respects individual autonomy.

The integration of AI and cognitive enhancement also sparks discussions about the nature of human identity and the potential transformation of societal norms.

As individuals gain access to tools that enhance memory, attention, or learning abilities, the definition of what it means to be "cognitively normal" may evolve.

Societal perceptions of intelligence, success, and achievement could be reshaped, necessitating ongoing dialogue about the ethical, social, and cultural implications of these transformations.

Neuroplasticity in the Digital Age

Neuroplasticity, the brain's ability to reorganize and adapt by forming new neural connections, is a concept that has gained renewed significance in the digital age.

As individuals increasingly engage with digital technologies, neuroplasticity plays a crucial role in shaping how our brains respond to and process information.

The constant exposure to digital stimuli, such as screens, notifications, and interactive content, has the potential to influence neural pathways and impact cognitive functions.

In the digital age, neuroplasticity is evident in the way individuals adapt to multitasking and information overload.

The brain adjusts to the demands of processing information from various sources simultaneously, leading to changes in attention spans, cognitive flexibility, and the ability to switch between tasks.

However, concerns have been raised about the potential negative effects of excessive digital stimulation on attention and cognitive performance, emphasizing the need for a nuanced understanding of how neuroplasticity operates in the context of the digital landscape.

The future of neuroplasticity in the digital age is intertwined with ongoing research and the development of technologies designed to harness its potential for positive outcomes.

Digital interventions, such as brain training apps and virtual reality experiences, aim to leverage neuroplasticity to enhance cognitive functions, improve memory, and support mental well-being.

These applications are designed to provide targeted stimuli that encourage adaptive changes in neural networks, reflecting a proactive approach to leveraging neuroplasticity for cognitive enhancement. Additionally, advancements in neurofeedback and brain-machine interfaces hold promise for personalized interventions that capitalize on neuroplasticity.

These technologies enable individuals to receive real-time feedback about their brain activity, allowing for targeted training to enhance specific cognitive functions.

The intersection of neuroscience and digital innovation offers the potential to develop increasingly sophisticated tools that empower individuals to shape and optimize their cognitive abilities.

However, ethical considerations accompany the future of neuroplasticity in the digital age as well. Questions about privacy, informed consent, and the potential societal implications of cognitive enhancement technologies need careful exploration.

As these technologies become more prevalent, establishing ethical guidelines and regulatory frameworks becomes essential to ensure responsible and equitable use.

Ethical Considerations and Societal Impacts

The potential future developments in technology, particularly those influencing the landscape of cognition, bring forth a myriad of ethical considerations and societal impacts.

As advancements in areas like artificial intelligence, brain-computer interfaces, and cognitive enhancement technologies continue to progress, it becomes imperative to navigate the ethical implications to ensure responsible and equitable integration into society.

One key ethical consideration revolves around issues of privacy and consent. Technologies that involve the monitoring or manipulation of cognitive processes often require access to sensitive personal information.

The collection and use of neural data raise concerns about the potential for unauthorized access, data breaches, and the commodification of individuals' thoughts and mental states.

Establishing robust privacy safeguards and obtaining informed consent from users become essential to protect the autonomy and rights of individuals in the cognitive technology landscape.

Another ethical concern relates to the potential for cognitive enhancements to create disparities in society.

As technologies emerge that can enhance memory, attention, or learning abilities, questions arise about access and equity. Will these enhancements be available to all, or will they be limited to privileged individuals or certain societal groups?

Striking a balance between providing access to cognitive enhancements and preventing the exacerbation of existing societal inequalities requires careful consideration and ethical frameworks.

The responsible use of cognitive technologies also involves addressing issues of bias and fairness.

If these technologies are trained on datasets that reflect societal biases, there is a risk of perpetuating and even exacerbating existing inequalities.

Ensuring that algorithms and models are developed and implemented with fairness and inclusivity in mind is crucial to avoid reinforcing discriminatory patterns and promoting just and equitable outcomes.

In the context of brain-computer interfaces, ethical considerations extend to questions of agency and autonomy.

As individuals gain the ability to control digital devices or communicate through thought alone, the potential for external influence or coercion becomes a concern.

Safeguarding the autonomy of individuals and ensuring that they have full control over the use of cognitive technologies is essential to prevent unintended consequences and protect users from potential abuses.

Societal impacts of cognitive technologies also include broader questions about human identity and the nature of being.

As these technologies advance, they may challenge conventional notions of cognition, intelligence, and what it means to be human.

Ethical discourse must involve societal reflections on the potential redefinition of human experiences, capabilities, and the ethical boundaries that should guide the integration of cognitive technologies into the fabric of society.

Cultivating Digital Well-being in the Future

Cultivating digital well-being in the future involves navigating the evolving landscape of technology with a holistic approach that prioritizes individuals' physical, mental, and emotional health.

As technology continues to advance, there are several key considerations and strategies for fostering digital well-being in the future:

1 **Digital Literacy and Empowerment:** Enhancing digital well-being starts with promoting digital literacy.

Educating individuals about responsible and mindful use of technology empowers them to navigate the digital world effectively.

Understanding how to critically evaluate information, manage screen time, and protect one's digital identity are essential components of digital literacy.

2 **Mindful Tech Practices:** Encouraging mindful tech practices involves incorporating principles of mindfulness into digital interactions.

This includes being present and intentional while using technology, practicing digital detoxes, and setting boundaries to prevent technology from becoming overwhelming.

Mindful tech practices can contribute to a healthier relationship with digital devices and platforms.

3 **User-Centric Design:** Future technologies should prioritize user well-being in their design. User-centric design principles can focus on creating interfaces and experiences that enhance usability while minimizing negative impacts on mental health.

Features that encourage breaks, limit notifications, and promote intentional use contribute to a more positive digital experience.

4 **Well-being Metrics and Monitoring:** Integrating well-being metrics into digital platforms allows users to monitor and understand their digital habits.

Apps and devices can provide insights into screen time, usage patterns, and the impact of digital interactions on mental health.

This information empowers individuals to make informed decisions about their digital engagement.

5 **Digital Detox Spaces:** Creating dedicated digital detox spaces or activities encourages individuals to take intentional breaks from technology.

Public spaces, workplaces, and even homes can incorporate areas where people can disconnect, fostering face-to-face interactions and moments of respite from the constant digital stimuli.

6 **Emotional Intelligence in AI:** As artificial intelligence becomes more prevalent, incorporating emotional intelligence into AI systems becomes crucial for digital well-being.

AI that understands and responds to human emotions appropriately can enhance user experiences and contribute to positive mental health outcomes.

7 **Community and Social Connection:** Emphasizing the role of technology in fostering genuine social connections is vital for digital well-being.

Future digital platforms should prioritize community-building, collaboration, and meaningful interactions, rather than solely focusing on metrics like likes and shares.

8 **Ethical Tech Practices:** Promoting ethical tech practices involves holding technology companies accountable for their impact on users' well-being.

This includes transparent data practices, ethical advertising, and responsible content moderation. Ethical tech practices contribute to a digital environment that prioritizes user health and safety.

9 **Digital Inclusivity:** Ensuring digital well-being for all requires addressing issues of digital inclusivity.

Future technologies should be designed to be accessible to diverse populations, considering factors such as age, ability, and socioeconomic status. Bridging the digital divide is essential for creating a more equitable digital landscape.

10 **Continued Research and Adaptation:** Cultivating digital well-being is an ongoing process that requires continuous research and adaptation.

Staying informed about the evolving impact of technology on well-being and adjusting strategies accordingly ensures that efforts to promote digital well-being remain effective in a dynamic technological landscape.

The future of the mind is intertwined with the trajectory of technological progress.

As we venture into uncharted territories of brain-computer interfaces, artificial intelligence, and immersive realities, it is crucial to approach these advancements with foresight, ethical consideration, and a commitment to preserving the core elements of our humanity.

The evolution of the future mind is a dynamic and multifaceted journey that invites collaboration, introspection, and responsible innovation to ensure a harmonious integration of technology and cognition in the years to come.

Conclusion

As we reach the final pages of "Digital Mindshift: How the Internet Rewires Our Brains," we find ourselves standing at the crossroads of the digital and the cerebral, witnessing the ongoing evolution of our cognitive landscape.

Throughout this exploration, we have uncovered the intricate ways in which the internet has left an indelible mark on the very fabric of our minds, reshaping our thoughts, behaviors, and perceptions in profound ways.

In the digital age, our attention spans have become both the currency and casualty of the information overload that defines our daily lives.

Yet, within this sea of stimuli, we have also witnessed the emergence of new forms of creativity and connectivity that transcend the limitations of physical boundaries.

The internet, with its vast networks and platforms, has become a powerful tool for collaboration, innovation, and the exchange of ideas on a global scale.

However, as we celebrate the positives, we must remain vigilant to the potential pitfalls that accompany the digital mindshift.

The addictive nature of social media, the erosion of privacy, and the challenges to critical thinking demand our attention and consideration.

It is in this delicate balance that we find ourselves tasked with navigating the complexities of the digital landscape while preserving the integrity of our cognitive well-being.

"Digital Mindshift" is a call to action, an invitation to engage thoughtfully with the technologies that shape our lives.

As we conclude this journey, let us carry forward a newfound awareness of the symbiotic relationship between our brains and the internet.

Let us embrace the responsibility to shape the digital future consciously, cultivating a harmonious coexistence that amplifies our human potential rather than diminishes it.

The digital mindshift is an ongoing process, and its trajectory is shaped by the choices we make today.

As we step away from these pages and back into the ever-evolving landscape of the internet, let us do so with a renewed sense of curiosity, resilience, and mindfulness.

The digital frontier beckons, and our minds are the compasses guiding us through uncharted territories. May we navigate this terrain with wisdom, adapting and evolving while preserving the essence of what makes us uniquely human.